Use of English

Ten practice tests for the **Cambridge C2 Proficiency**

Michael Macdonald

PROSPERITY EDUCATION

PROSPERITY EDUCATION

www.prosperityeducation.net

Registered offices: Sherlock Close, Cambridge
CB3 0HP, United Kingdom

© Prosperity Education Ltd. 2020

First published 2020
Revised edition published 2021

ISBN: 978-1-91-612973-3

Manufactured on demand by Kindle Direct Publishing.

Cover design and typesetting by ORP Cambridge

For further information and resources, visit:
www.prosperityeducation.net

To infinity and beyond.

Contents

Introduction

Welcome to this second edition of sample tests for the Cambridge C2 Proficiency, Use of English (Parts 1–4).

The pass threshold of the Cambridge C2 Proficiency (CPE) examination is 60% and so, in order to allow ample time for the reading parts (Parts 5–8) of Paper 1, it is advisable that candidates complete The Use of English section (Parts 1–4) as quickly as possible while maintaining accuracy. For instance, completing each part in fewer than five minutes will allow 55 minutes in which to complete the reading parts.

This resource comprises ten whole Use of English tests, answer keys, write-in answer sheets and a marking scheme, allowing you to score each test out of 36 marks.

The content has been written to closely replicate the Cambridge exam experience, and has undergone comprehensive expert and peer review. You or your students, if you are a teacher, will hopefully enjoy the wide range of essay topics and benefit from the repetitive practice, something that is key to preparing for this part of the C2 Proficiency (CPE) examination.

For me, having prepared many students for this and other Cambridge exams, pre- and post-2015, when the specification changed, this is clearly the section that poses the biggest challenge. Without there being much support available by way of quality practice material, students struggle to gain the necessary levels of confidence in the Use of English section prior to sitting the exam. Therefore, in my classes, after studying and working through the core knowledge required, we drill, drill and drill exercises in preparation for the exams.

I hope that you will find this resource a useful study aid, and I wish you all the best in preparing for the exam.

Michael Macdonald
Madrid, 2020

About the C2 Proficiency exam

The Use of English section of the C2 Proficiency (CPE) exam is broken down into four parts:

Part 1. Multiple choice cloze	
What is being tested?	This part of the exam mostly tests vocabulary, idioms, collocations, shades of meaning, phrasal verbs, complementation, semantic precision and fixed phrases.
How does it work?	It contains a test with eight gaps, each gap prompting multiple-choice questions. Each question has four possible answers, only one of which is correct.
How is it marked?	One mark is awarded for each correct answer.

Part 2. Open cloze	
What is being tested?	This part of the exam has a lexico-grammatical focus, testing candidates' awareness and control of grammar, fixed phrasing, collocation, semantic precision and, to an extent, vocabulary (the particles/prepositions for phrasal verbs).
How does it work?	It contains a text with eight gaps, each gap representing a missing word. No hints are given: candidates must think of the correct word for each gap.
How is it marked?	One mark is awarded for each correct answer.

Part 3. Word formation	
What is being tested?	This part of the exam focuses on affixation, internal changes and compounding in word formation, and vocabulary.
How does it work?	It contains a text with eight gaps, each gap representing a missing word. Beside each gap is a 'prompt' word that must be altered in some way to complete the sentence correctly.
How is it marked?	One mark is awarded for each correct answer.

Part 4. Key word transformations	
What is being tested?	This part of the exam has a lexico-grammatical focus, testing lexis, grammar and vocabulary.
How does it work?	It contains six sentences, each followed by a 'key' word and an alternative sentence conveying the same meaning as the first but with a gap in the middle. Candidates are to use the keyword provided to complete the second sentence so that it has a similar meaning to the first sentence. Candidates cannot change the keyword provided.
How is it marked?	Each correct answer is broken down into two marks.

Cambridge C2 Proficiency Use of English

Test 1

For questions 1–8, read the text below and decide which answer best fits each gap. In the separate answer sheet, mark the appropriate answer (A, B, C or D).

The bicycle

The 'safety bicycle' of the late 19th century **(1)**_____ a much closer resemblance to a modern bike than its predecessors. The 'Penny Farthing', which gained its name due to its giant front wheel, its rather tiny rear wheel, and their comparative sizes being similar to the penny and farthing coins in the UK at the time, was for all **(2)**_____ and purposes a vehicle designed for racing. A brave rider would **(3)**_____ at the top of the 150cm-high front wheel. This device had in turn **(4)**_____ Pierre Lallemont's 'Velocipede', a vehicle that featured a rotary crank mechanism to turn the wheels, according to his American patent in 1866. However, it still lacked a chain drive and a 'true' gearing system, and, rather worryingly, any kind of brake.

(5)_____ the Penny Farthing had been ridden almost exclusively by daring young men, the safety bike could be used by anyone and quite a scandal was **(6)**_____ up by one newspaper around the time of the bike's commercial launch when it reported on young women riding the bikes, unchaperoned, around the city of New York. What is more – these trailblazing ladies had also dared to wear trousers – a **(7)**_____ outrage in some parts of society. In fact, Susan B. Antony, a 19th-century women's activist, claimed that bicycling had done more to emancipate women than any one thing in the world.

The bicycle has continued to be an understated symbol of innovation and evolution, if nothing else **(8)**_____ the way to ease of movement for many, and in an undoubtedly environmentally friendly way.

1	**A** takes	**B** gives	**C** bears	**D** makes
2	**A** intends	**B** intents	**C** insights	**D** intakes
3	**A** clamber	**B** perch	**C** climb	**D** swing
4	**A** superseded	**B** circumvented	**C** overcome	**D** overhauled
5	**A** However	**B** Whereas	**C** Whenever	**D** Since
6	**A** stirred	**B** twisted	**C** mixed	**D** shaken
7	**A** doubtless	**B** veritable	**C** factual	**D** genuine
8	**A** beginning	**B** starting	**C** opening	**D** launching

For questions 9–16, read the text below and decide which word best fits each gap. Use only one word for each gap. In the separate answer sheet, write your answers in capital letters, using one box per letter.

The first Apple Mac

Competing fiercely **(9)**_____ a share of the emerging home-computer market in 1979, a successful young company called Apple was developing its Lisa computer, the second commercial machine **(10)**_____ utilise a Graphic User Interface (GUI). The engineers at Apple knew that success **(11)**_____ in being able to precisely render an image visible on screen onto a printed page **(12)**_____ being confined to just one printer, and the company's founding executive, the late Steve Jobs, had in the Lisa a product that he knew could change the world of office communications. **(13)** _____, it was to be the Lisa's successor, the seminal Macintosh, that would ultimately change that world.

The Apple Macintosh computer was launched in January 1984 through a high-profile marketing **(14)**_____ that deployed an advert directed by Ridley Scott and a national premiere during the half- **(15)**_____ break of that year's Superbowl, the USA's most popular televised sporting event. Priced at $2,495, it was the first commercially available desktop computer with a GUI and mouse, and its acknowledged potential amongst the design and graphical arts communities was profound. The **(16)**_____, as they say, is history.

For questions 17–24, use the stem word on the right to form the correct word that fills each gap. In the separate answer sheet, write your answers in capital letters, using one box per letter.

Animal hybrids

Animal hybrids – the **(17)**_____ of two different species of animal – are more common than you might suspect. Probably the best-known hybrid is the mule, which is the product of a female horse and a male donkey. Mules are prized for their stamina and **(18)**_____.   **SPRING**

STRONG

Although mules are famously unable to bear young, it is a myth that all hybrids are **(19)**_____. Some populations are bred in great numbers, often for food production. One useful result of **(20)**_____ is the 'beefalo' (the result of mixing domesticated cows and wild buffalo), which is bred purely for the production of beef.   **FERTILITY**

BREED

And there can be definite advantages to hybridisation in the wild, too. While some hybrids display **(21)**_____ characteristics halfway between those of their parents, others can have unexpected advantages, making them better able to deal with predators or a changing environment.   **ANATOMY**

Some hybrids are only possible in **(22)**_____, because the animals would never encounter each other in the wild. 'Ligers', for instance, are a mix of lion and tiger, and are the largest feline, with one specimen **(23)**_____ in at an incredible 418.2kg.   **CAPTIVE**

WEIGHT

Often, of course, hybrids become new species in their own right. **(24)**_____ often identify 'hybrid swarms', where hybrids and 'pure' individuals are completely mixed.   **CONSERVE**

For questions 25–30, complete the second sentence, using the word given, so that it has a similar meaning to the first sentence. Do not change the word provided and use between three and eight words in total. In the separate answer sheet, write your answers in capital letters, using one box per letter.

25   The teacher was not very clear when he spoke at times.

   LACK

   At times _____ the teacher spoke.

26   They had difficulty in deciding due to the huge choice.

   REACH

   The huge range made _____ a decision.

27   Despite his run of bad luck, Stuart still thought he could win the game.

   HOPE

   Stuart refused to give _____ his recent run of bad luck.

28   The weather forecast says it will probably rain tonight.

   STRONG

   The weather forecast says that _____ rain tonight.

29   The manager didn't think it was reasonable of you to complain so much about the hotel room.

   JUSTIFIED

   The manager didn't think you _____ a fuss about the service.

30   There would have been no problems yesterday had Sebastian not interfered.

   SMOOTHLY

   Without Sebastian's _____ yesterday.

Answer sheet: Cambridge C2 Proficiency
Use of English

Test No. ☐

Mark out of 36 ☐

Name _____   **Date** _____

Part 1: Multiple choice

8 marks

Mark the appropriate answer (A, B, C or D).

| 0 | A | B | C | D | |

1	A	B	C	D			5	A	B	C	D	
2	A	B	C	D			6	A	B	C	D	
3	A	B	C	D			7	A	B	C	D	
4	A	B	C	D			8	A	B	C	D	

Part 2: Open cloze

8 marks

Write your answers in capital letters, using one box per letter.

| 0 | B | E | C | A | U | S | E | | | | |

9											
10											
11											
12											
13											
14											
15											
16											

Part 3: Word formation

8 marks

Write your answers in capital letters, using one box per letter.

17 | | | | | | | | | | |
18 | | | | | | | | | | |
19 | | | | | | | | | | |
20 | | | | | | | | | | |
21 | | | | | | | | | | |
22 | | | | | | | | | | |
23 | | | | | | | | | | |
24 | | | | | | | | | | |

Part 4: Key word transformation

12 marks

Write your answers in capital letters, using one box per letter.

25 | | | | | | | | | | | | | | | | | |
26 | | | | | | | | | | | | | | | | | |
27 | | | | | | | | | | | | | | | | | |
28 | | | | | | | | | | | | | | | | | |
29 | | | | | | | | | | | | | | | | | |
30 | | | | | | | | | | | | | | | | | |

Cambridge C2 Proficiency Use of English

Test 2

For questions 1–8, read the text below and decide which answer best fits each gap. In the separate answer sheet, mark the appropriate answer (A, B, C or D).

Power naps

The *siesta* has long been a characteristic of Spanish life. A short sleep in the middle of the day seems an **(1)**_____ concept, an impossible luxury. Lately though, the expression 'power nap' has become common in an international Anglo-Saxon word **(2)**_____ to describe, fundamentally, the same thing.

Siestas, though, seem to be the territory of the relaxed Hispanics, long sleepy afternoons and even longer evenings. Power-naps, as the name might **(3)**_____, are the terrain of Silicon Valley execs, eager students and go-getters. So what **(4)**_____ a *siesta* or power nap? It is generally agreed this must last between 10 and 25 minutes – any more and you might enter **(5)**_____ sleep, which is much more difficult to awake from quickly). When it comes to power-naps there is no need to sleep in a bed, or even in a horizontal position. One might have one in the busiest of situations – subway trains or an office – and they can take place at any time. Try it for yourself and you´ll be amazed by just how much it **(6)**_____ you up!

Siestas, on the other hand, usually take place after a **(7)**_____ lunch, in a bed or sofa, or the likes, and preferably in a cool, dark environment.

Everyone has their own favourite way of catching 40 **(8)**_____ and the fact is that power-nap practitioners report feeling less tired and improved awareness as a result.

1	A	unconvincing	B	implausible	C	imported	D	inconclusive
2	A	pool	B	puddle	C	bank	D	pot
3	A	surmise	B	deduce	C	entail	D	imply
4	A	constitutes	B	does	C	appoints	D	ordains
5	A	profound	B	immersed	C	acute	D	deep
6	A	hits	B	pulls	C	perks	D	lifts
7	A	solid	B	hearty	C	strong	D	robust
8	A	blinks	B	winks	C	minutes	D	instants

For questions 9–16, read the text below and decide which word best fits each gap. Use only one word for each gap. In the separate answer sheet, write your answers in capital letters, using one box per letter.

Commuting

Commuting – that is, to (9)_____ travelling from one region to another to work before travelling back to where you live on a regular basis – has been possible since the advent of the railway. However, in recent times it has become the (10)_____ as opposed to the exception, as people increasingly move out of the cities and into more suburban settings.

Let's (11)_____ London as an example. Most people who work in what is considered to be the central part of the city must commute due to the excessive cost of living in (12)_____ a place. A journey of at least one hour on public transport is by no (13)_____ uncommon, as the use of private cars has been reduced greatly by anti-pollution and congestion legislation.

On the more extreme side of things are stories of business people traveling up to three hours (14)_____ way every day rather than living in the capital city. You might expect that these journeys would be made by train, but recently the lower cost of air travel has made it widely possible for people with relatively normal incomes to travel from the (15)_____ of Barcelona to London or Zurich, for example, thus (16)_____ advantage of the higher standard of living and better weather of their home city while earning a higher salary obtainable in one of those financial hubs.

For questions 17–24, use the stem word on the right to form the correct word that fills each gap. In the separate answer sheet, write your answers in capital letters, using one box per letter.

The chupacabra

The chupacabra, or *chupacabras*, is a blood-thirsty, mystery creature, **(17)**_____ responsible for killing sheep and goats. It occupies the same space between reality and myth that is occupied by creatures such as the Yeti, the Loch Ness Monster and mermaids, with one difference – it is a **(18)**_____ new monster.

SUPPOSE

RELATE

The creature was first reported as late as 1995 on the island of Puerto Rico in the Caribbean, but **(19)**_____ have since spread to South America, the United States and, most recently, Russia and Southern Europe. If the chupacabra is real, it has an impressive range for a wild animal. The **(20)**_____ expert on the *chupacabras* calls it 'the first internet monster', attributing the rapid spread of reports to Google.

SEE

FORE

As with most monsters, there is precious little physical evidence, and eyewitness reports are sketchy and often contradictory, and it has, of course, **(21)**_____ avoided capture.

MYSTERY

Some evidence for the creature's **(22)**_____ comes from its diet. The name 'chupacabra' literally translates as 'goat sucker', because it apparently drains its victims of blood. Dead sheep have been connected with *chupacabras* reports from its earliest **(23)**_____ in the media. However, scientific analyses of these creatures reveal that dogs or coyotes are the likeliest culprits.

EXIST

APPEAR

So it seems as though the *chupacabras* is **(24)**_____ a case of mistaken identity. But, as with all good monsters, the stories won't go away…

ESSENCE

For questions 25–30, complete the second sentence, using the word given, so that it has a similar meaning to the first sentence. Do not change the word provided and use between three and eight words in total. In the separate answer sheet, write your answers in capital letters, using one box per letter.

25   They took the decision to stop playing after it got dark.

    FELL

    Not until _____ stop playing.

26   You can only fish in the park if you have a permit.

    RESTRICTED

    Fishing _____ you have a permit.

27   Her daughter said the portrait looked nothing like her mother.

    RESEMBLANCE

    The mother was told by her daughter _____ her.

28   The concert would have been held outdoors, but it rained.

    PLACE

    If it _____ inside.

29   Barry is faced with many problems during his working week.

    CONTEND

    Barry has a _____ during his working week.

30   Mr Smart was careful not to get into the position whereby he might lose all his money.

    POSSIBILITY

    Mr Smart didn't expose _____ all his money.

Answer sheet: Cambridge C2 Proficiency Use of English

Test No. ☐

Mark out of 36 ☐

Name _____   **Date** _____

Part 1: Multiple choice   8 marks

Mark the appropriate answer (A, B, C or D).

| 0 | A | B ▬ | C | D |

1	A	B	C	D		5	A	B	C	D
2	A	B	C	D		6	A	B	C	D
3	A	B	C	D		7	A	B	C	D
4	A	B	C	D		8	A	B	C	D

Part 2: Open cloze   8 marks

Write your answers in capital letters, using one box per letter.

| 0 | B | E | C | A | U | S | E | | | | |

9										
10										
11										
12										
13										
14										
15										
16										

Part 3: Word formation

Write your answers in capital letters, using one box per letter.

17 ☐☐☐☐☐☐☐☐☐☐☐

18 ☐☐☐☐☐☐☐☐☐☐☐

19 ☐☐☐☐☐☐☐☐☐☐☐

20 ☐☐☐☐☐☐☐☐☐☐☐

21 ☐☐☐☐☐☐☐☐☐☐☐

22 ☐☐☐☐☐☐☐☐☐☐☐

23 ☐☐☐☐☐☐☐☐☐☐☐

24 ☐☐☐☐☐☐☐☐☐☐☐

Part 4: Key word transformation

12 marks

Write your answers in capital letters, using one box per letter.

25 ☐☐☐☐☐☐☐☐☐☐☐☐☐☐☐☐
☐☐☐☐☐☐☐☐☐☐☐☐☐☐☐☐

26 ☐☐☐☐☐☐☐☐☐☐☐☐☐☐☐☐
☐☐☐☐☐☐☐☐☐☐☐☐☐☐☐☐

27 ☐☐☐☐☐☐☐☐☐☐☐☐☐☐☐☐
☐☐☐☐☐☐☐☐☐☐☐☐☐☐☐☐

28 ☐☐☐☐☐☐☐☐☐☐☐☐☐☐☐☐
☐☐☐☐☐☐☐☐☐☐☐☐☐☐☐☐

29 ☐☐☐☐☐☐☐☐☐☐☐☐☐☐☐☐
☐☐☐☐☐☐☐☐☐☐☐☐☐☐☐☐

30 ☐☐☐☐☐☐☐☐☐☐☐☐☐☐☐☐
☐☐☐☐☐☐☐☐☐☐☐☐☐☐☐☐

Cambridge C2 Proficiency Use of English

Test 3

For questions 1–8, read the text below and decide which answer best fits each gap. In the separate answer sheet, mark the appropriate answer (A, B, C or D).

Plastic problems

Environmentalists are **(1)**_____ with governments across the length and **(2)**_____ of the planet to introduce legislation that will **(3)**_____ the huge amount to plastic used by us as a society – eight-million tonnes of which is disposed of every year in landfill sites and the oceans without being recycled. The planet is literally being poisoned and suffocated by the human race.

Some plastics take thousands of years to **(4)**_____. Recently, birds' eggs in The Arctic have been found to contain plastic micro fibres, showing **(5)**_____ that the material has entered the food chain of the planet's inhabitants, with no telling of the long-term consequences.

(6)_____ action is required at a global governmental level. Consumers are being discouraged from using single-use plastics through taxation on things like plastic bags. However, it is at an industrial level that the attractiveness of plastic as a cheap and convenient means of packaging needs to be **(7)**_____.

(8)_____ a sea change in attitudes and actions, we are surely heading for a catastrophic environmental situation in the very near future, even if it is one that could be said to have a slow burn.

1	**A**	beseeching	**B**	pleading	**C**	begging	**D**	imploring
2	**A**	width	**B**	breadth	**C**	depth	**D**	height
3	**A**	combat	**B**	counteract	**C**	hinder	**D**	resist
4	**A**	break off	**B**	break up	**C**	break down	**D**	break out
5	**A**	definitely	**B**	surely	**C**	conclusively	**D**	rightly
6	**A**	Resolute	**B**	Harsh	**C**	Decisive	**D**	Definitive
7	**A**	sent	**B**	addressed	**C**	directed	**D**	pitched
8	**A**	Notwithstanding	**B**	Albeit	**C**	Nevertheless	**D**	Regarding

For questions 9–16, read the text below and decide which word best fits each gap. Use only one word for each gap. In the separate answer sheet, write your answers in capital letters, using one box per letter.

Driverless cars

Imagine travelling on a crowded motorway filled with cars travelling at around 100 kilometres per hour – with just a couple of metres **(9)**_____ each car. Sounds nightmarish, doesn't it? But this could be the reality of your **(10)**_____ commute in just a few years' time.

When you arrive at work, you won't be hunting for a parking space and paying for the privilege of leaving your vehicle in the street. **(11)**_____, you'll wave it goodbye and another car will be along to **(12)**_____ you up when you're ready to return home.

According to its proponents, the rise of the driverless vehicle will **(13)**_____ in faster, safer, less stressful and cheaper car travel. The optimists predict that it won't be long before we are using them regularly. Elon Musk thinks they could be a commercial reality by the 2020s, while BMW and Ford have both said they expect to see companies buying entire **(14)**_____ of driverless vehicles by 2021!

There will be a complete change in the way we view the ownership of cars. Rather than buying a personal car, we will buy **(15)**_____ pay-as-you-go services – meaning big savings in terms of insurance, car tax and maintenance. Our cars sit **(16)**_____ for most of the time – just imagine not paying for all those hours when your car is not being used.

For questions 17–24, use the stem word on the right to form the correct word that fills each gap. In the separate answer sheet, write your answers in capital letters, using one box per letter.

History's most influential obscure scientist

"The world has used me so **(17)**_____, I fear it has made me suspicious of everyone."   **KIND**

These were the words of one of Victorian England's most **(18)**_____ scientific researchers, a paleontologist and fossil collector who spent a lifetime hunting for finds in southern England. Their knowledge and **(19)**_____ did much to influence geological thinking.   **INNOVATE**

SEE

The researcher had unlikely beginnings: one of ten children, **(20)**_____ in 1799 to a carpenter and his wife in the small coastal town of Lyme Regis, with a limited education and few opportunities to read widely. However, the father's sideline – selling fossils to tourists – gave the young geologist a head start in practical science. Their family shop was known throughout Europe as a mecca for **(21)**_____ collectors and enthusiasts.   **BEAR**

COUNT

The rough seas along England's south coast often cause landslides, revealing fossils. Collecting them quickly can be dangerous work. However, this often **(22)**_____ and difficult research has led to some amazing **(23)**_____: ichthyosaurs, plesiosaurs and pterosaurs.   **COMFORT**

DISCOVER

And yet, with all this experience, this researcher was denied membership of the eminent Geological Society of London, and their research appeared only once in scientific journals during their lifetime. What was the reason for this **(24)**_____? Mary Anning was a woman.   **OBSCURE**

For questions 25–30, complete the second sentence, using the word given, so that it has a similar meaning to the first sentence. Do not change the word provided and use between three and eight words in total. In the separate answer sheet, write your answers in capital letters, using one box per letter.

25   The thing I love doing most is playing the guitar.

   MORE

   There is _____ the guitar.

26   If the doctor had not called the ambulance so swiftly the man would have died.

   IN

   But for _____ the man would have died.

27   There is a possibility that this species of cat will become extinct.

   DANGER

   This species of cat _____ extinct.

28   When he was interviewed, the famous singer did not mention how his first teacher had influenced him.

   REFERENCE

   The famous singer _____ of his first teacher in the interview.

29   The audience suddenly started to applaud loudly.

   SUDDEN

   All _____ of applause from the audience.

30   The manager said that he had paid attention to my complaints and would take the appropriate action.

   NOTE

   The manager said that he had _____ accordingly.

Answer sheet: Cambridge C2 Proficiency Use of English

Test No. ☐

Mark out of 36 ☐

Name _____   **Date** _____

Part 1: Multiple choice

8 marks

Mark the appropriate answer (A, B, C or D).

0	A	B	C	D

1	A	B	C	D		5	A	B	C	D
2	A	B	C	D		6	A	B	C	D
3	A	B	C	D		7	A	B	C	D
4	A	B	C	D		8	A	B	C	D

Part 2: Open cloze

8 marks

Write your answers in capital letters, using one box per letter.

0	B	E	C	A	U	S	E				

9											
10											
11											
12											
13											
14											
15											
16											

Part 3: Word formation

8 marks

Write your answers in capital letters, using one box per letter.

| 17 | | | | | | | | | | | |

| 18 | | | | | | | | | | | |

| 19 | | | | | | | | | | | |

| 20 | | | | | | | | | | | |

| 21 | | | | | | | | | | | |

| 22 | | | | | | | | | | | |

| 23 | | | | | | | | | | | |

| 24 | | | | | | | | | | | |

Part 4: Key word transformation

12 marks

Write your answers in capital letters, using one box per letter.

| 25 | | | | | | | | | | | | | | | | | | |
| | | | | | | | | | | | | | | | | | | |

| 26 | | | | | | | | | | | | | | | | | | |
| | | | | | | | | | | | | | | | | | | |

| 27 | | | | | | | | | | | | | | | | | | |
| | | | | | | | | | | | | | | | | | | |

| 28 | | | | | | | | | | | | | | | | | | |
| | | | | | | | | | | | | | | | | | | |

| 29 | | | | | | | | | | | | | | | | | | |
| | | | | | | | | | | | | | | | | | | |

| 30 | | | | | | | | | | | | | | | | | | |
| | | | | | | | | | | | | | | | | | | |

Cambridge C2 Proficiency Use of English

Test 4

___

For questions 1–8, read the text below and decide which answer best fits each gap. In the separate answer sheet, mark the appropriate answer (A, B, C or D).

Hypertext Markup Language (HTML)

A derivative of SGML (Standard Generalized Markup Language), HTML, which **(1)**_____ Hypertext Markup Language was originally developed in the early 1990s at the European Organization for Nuclear Research (CERN) laboratories, Switzerland, by Tim Berners-Lee, the person **(2)**_____ with creating the internet.

Put simply, it brought the coding of content to the internet by defining the information structure of web pages, **(3)**_____ creating the World Wide Web. Yet, unlike SGML, HTML is **(4)**_____ more with formatting than structure. In fact, HTML is just one application of SGML containing comparatively fewer 'tags' that are recognisable by all web browsers. By **(5)**_____ 'hypertext' links within its structure, HTML includes a referential feature, **(6)**_____ the reader to move between HTML files, images, and other multimedia programmes across the net.

A reason why **(7)**_____ markup such as HTML is necessary for presenting content in web pages is that the content must be device-independent. For example, variables like line breaks and font size are ultimately **(8)**_____ by the width of a browser's window or the viewing device's screen.

1	**A** stands for	**B** sits for	**C** appears for	**D** answers for
2	**A** credited	**B** invented	**C** ascribed	**D** recognised
3	**A** basically	**B** ultimately	**C** finally	**D** conclusively
4	**A** concerned	**B** concentrated	**C** interested	**D** affiliated
5	**A** entwining	**B** embedding	**C** ingraining	**D** encompassing
6	**A** empowering	**B** enabling	**C** implementing	**D** licensing
7	**A** correction	**B** generic	**C** mixed	**D** collective
8	**A** decided	**B** arbitrated	**C** resolved	**D** determined

For questions 9–16, read the text below and decide which word best fits each gap. Use only one word for each gap. In the separate answer sheet, write your answers in capital letters, using one box per letter.

Making a difference

You should **(9)**_____ believe that you are too young to make a difference to the planet. **(10)**_____, as an example, a 14-year-old school student from Pittsburgh in the USA, Suvir Mirchandani. Suvir was perhaps a little more environmentally aware than his peers. He certainly showed initiative, persistence and innovation in his approach to reducing waste. His school, like most, produced huge numbers of worksheets, fliers and letters home to parents. Of course, many people complained **(11)**_____ the amount of paper that was being used, but Suvir went one **(12)**_____ further. He wondered whether switching fonts would make a difference to the amount of ink used by the school, and he set out to discover which font was the most eco-friendly.

He looked at the five most commonly used characters in English, enlarged them, printed them onto card and cut them **(13)**_____. He did this in four of the common computer fonts (Garamond, Times New Roman, Century Gothic and Comic Sans). Weighing the size of each letter, he calculated that his school could reduce its ink consumption by 24% – simply by switching to the thinner letters of Garamond. He claimed that this would represent a saving of an incredible $21,000 per annum.

(14)_____ further thought, Suvir made more ambitious claims, estimating that a similar switch could save the US Federal Government $136 million. His ideas grabbed the headlines, although further analysis undermined his bold claims. Many pointed out that switching to paperless communication would save **(15)**_____ ink and paper. However, his ideas certainly succeeded in focusing attention **(16)**_____ one small change that could make a big difference: an impressive feat for a teenager.

For questions 17–24, use the stem word on the right to form the correct word that fills each gap. In the separate answer sheet, write your answers in capital letters, using one box per letter.

Lady Gaga

Lady Gaga is an American singer, song-writer, and actress. She is one of the best-selling recording artists in history, was nominated for an Oscar for her performance in the film 'A Star is Born', and won an Oscar for the film's **(17)**_____.   **SOUND**

Her **(18)**_____ dress-sense – Gaga wore an   **RAGE**
outfit made of meat to the 2010 MTV Awards – has also
won her **(19)**_____ from the US fashion   **RECOGNISE**
industry.

Gaga, real name Stefani Germanotta, was born in 1986
in New York and began learning to play the piano at an
early age. By her teens she was performing regularly.
Her **(20)**_____ album was 2008's 'The   **BREAK**
Fame', featuring her hit song 'Poker Face'.

Her vocal style shows incredible **(21)**_____   **VERSATILE**
and her albums have ranged **(22)**_____ from   **STYLE**
electronic pop to easy listening. She has always focused
on the visual aspects of performance and her videos are
often more like short films. Her live shows are also
famously **(23)**_____ and often controversial.   **INNOVATE**

But Gaga is not just a performer. Her
(24)_____ organisation Born This Way
campaigns for young people and funds anti-bullying   **PHILANTHROPY**
projects, and she is a prominent advocate of LGBT
causes.

For questions 25–30, complete the second sentence, using the word given, so that it has a similar meaning to the first sentence. Do not change the word provided and use between three and eight words in total. In the separate answer sheet, write your answers in capital letters, using one box per letter.

25   The children ignored me no matter how loudly I shouted.

TOOK

Even though I _____ me.

26   It is very probable that it will rain tomorrow.

EVERY

There _____ tomorrow.

27   Claire and Simon don't agree about what is best for their children.

DIFFERENCE

Claire and Simon _____ concerning what is best for their children.

28   It was a great surprise to us when Alaina arrived punctually yesterday.

ARRIVAL

Alaina took _____ yesterday.

29   Jake was very important when the proposal was drafted.

INSTRUMENTAL

Jake was _____ of the proposal.

30   Her behaviour at the conference gave her the bad reputation she now has.

CONDUCTED

The way she _____ her being held in ill repute.

Answer sheet: Cambridge C2 Proficiency Use of English

Test No. ☐

Mark out of 36 ☐

Name _____   **Date** _____

Part 1: Multiple choice
8 marks

Mark the appropriate answer (A, B, C or D).

| 0 | A | **B** | C | D |

1	A	B	C	D		5	A	B	C	D
2	A	B	C	D		6	A	B	C	D
3	A	B	C	D		7	A	B	C	D
4	A	B	C	D		8	A	B	C	D

Part 2: Open cloze
8 marks

Write your answers in capital letters, using one box per letter.

| 0 | B | E | C | A | U | S | E | | | | |

9											
10											
11											
12											
13											
14											
15											
16											

Part 3: Word formation

8 marks

Write your answers in capital letters, using one box per letter.

17

18

19

20

21

22

23

24

Part 4: Key word transformation

12 marks

Write your answers in capital letters, using one box per letter.

25

26

27

28

29

30

Cambridge C2 Proficiency Use of English

Test 5

For questions 1–8, read the text below and decide which answer best fits each gap. In the separate answer sheet, mark the appropriate answer (A, B, C or D).

Recording music at home

The release and **(1)**_____ Number 1 smash hit 'Your Woman' by one-man-band 'White Town' in 1997 undeniably proved that you could actually write, record, release and achieve success as a musical **(2)**_____ industry. Using an 8-track recording device, Jyoti Mishra recorded the song in his **(3)**_____ room in Derby, England. He played it to his girlfriend, who encouraged him to do something with it. He could only afford to have five copies made, however, and so he sent one of them to Radio One, which soon started playing it, and the song became the most requested track of the week. As a direct consequence, he **(4)**_____ a deal with EMI. When it was released, it shot to Number 1 in the charts. Mishra **(5)**_____ refused to appear in a video or on British TV to promote it, yet it sold 165,000 copies during the first week.

Since the **(6)**_____ of powerful home computers, home recording of music has become a very popular hobby for musical enthusiasts, as well as an outlet for **(7)**_____ producers. No longer are expensive recording studios the only option for prospective music producers. **(8)**_____, a well-equipped home studio, a few instruments and a whole lot of time, talent and energy are what you need if you want to write the next big hit!

1	A	following	B	posterior	C	consecutive	D	subsequent
2	A	cottage	B	bungalow	C	farm	D	house
3	A	extra	B	spare	C	back up	D	empty
4	A	landed	B	took off	C	pitched	D	hooked
5	A	completely	B	point-blank	C	utterly	D	surely
6	A	advent	B	evolution	C	revolution	D	formulation
7	A	budding	B	developing	C	blooming	D	possible
8	A	Furthermore	B	Nonetheless	C	Rather	D	Nevertheless

For questions 9–16, read the text below and decide which word best fits each gap. Use only one word for each gap. In the separate answer sheet, write your answers in capital letters, using one box per letter.

News International *

(9)_____ the year 2000, the Australian media mogul Rupert Murdoch's global business empire comprised more than 800 companies and boasted a (10)_____ worth of $5 billion.

(11)_____ to the seemingly brutal, monopolistic nature of his ambitions, his career has been the (12)_____ of much criticism, with perhaps the most bitter episode occurring in 1986 when his News International organisation, (13)_____ then included British newspapers the *Sun*, *News of The World*, *The Times* and the *Sunday Times*), controversially relocated its London printing business from Fleet Street to Wapping, replacing traditional letterpress printing (14)_____ new 'phototypesetting' technology.

The process famously saw the sacking of some 5,000 striking employees (15)_____ losing a single day's production.

(16)_____ to Linda Melvern in her book, *The End of The Street*, Murdoch characterised the manufacturing aspect of the industry in 1985 as "three times the number of jobs at five times the level of wages".

* News International was a publishing empire that encompassed some of the UK's most popular newspapers, and formed part of a larger international conglomerate.

For questions 17–24, use the stem word on the right to form the correct word that fills each gap. In the separate answer sheet, write your answers in capital letters, using one box per letter.

Motor Neurone Disease

There is no **(17)**_____ cause of Motor Neurone Disease (MND), nor is there a cure, and its symptoms affect sufferers in different ways. Furthermore, the rate at which the disease progresses is difficult to determine. **(18)**_____, for anyone who has the **(19)**_____ to have it, the **(20)**_____ is terminal.

KNOW

TRAGEDY

FORTUNE

PROGNOSE

Put simply, the disease slowly interrupts the electrical messages sent by synapses in the brain to the muscles, causing the sufferer to experience **(21)**_____ less mobility as time goes on. One by one, the synapses cease to transmit their messages and, **(22)**_____, the muscles stop working.

INCREASE

CONSEQUENCE

Researchers suspect that there may be a link between MND and physical trauma, with studies performed on rugby players producing evidence that players who experienced repeated concussions during their playing careers have a **(23)**_____ chance of developing the disease in later life. While this theory divides the scientific community, scientists are agreed that there is **(24)**_____ no real known cause for the disease.

HEIGHT

PRESENT

For questions 25–30, complete the second sentence, using the word given, so that it has a similar meaning to the first sentence. Do not change the word provided and use between three and eight words in total. In the separate answer sheet, write your answers in capital letters, using one box per letter.

25   Jake was forced to accept what the council decided.

      CHOICE

      Jake _____ of the council.

26   Pupils are absolutely forbidden from using the teachers' toilets.

      ACCOUNT

      On _____ teachers' toilets.

27   Jackie's friend suggested that she ignored the cruel children in her class.

      ATTENTION

      Jackie's friend advised _____ the cruel children in her class.

28   The thing I'd like most would be to see Mohammed again.

      MORE

      There's _____ see Mohammed again.

29   If you had not changed our original agreement, everything would have been fine.

      STUCK

      Had _____ agreed, everything would have been fine.

30   In Susan's opinion she hasn't done anything she should apologise for.

      CONCERNED

      As _____ nothing for which an apology is deserved.

Name _____   **Date** _____

Part 1: Multiple choice   8 marks

Mark the appropriate answer (A, B, C or D).

0	A	**B**	C	D

1	A	B	C	D		5	A	B	C	D
2	A	B	C	D		6	A	B	C	D
3	A	B	C	D		7	A	B	C	D
4	A	B	C	D		8	A	B	C	D

Part 2: Open cloze   8 marks

Write your answers in capital letters, using one box per letter.

0	B	E	C	A	U	S	E				

9											
10											
11											
12											
13											
14											
15											
16											

Part 3: Word formation

8 marks

Write your answers in capital letters, using one box per letter.

17

18

19

20

21

22

23

24

Part 4: Key word transformation

12 marks

Write your answers in capital letters, using one box per letter.

25

26

27

28

29

30

Cambridge C2 Proficiency Use of English

Test 6

For questions 1–8, read the text below and decide which answer best fits each gap. In the separate answer sheet, mark the appropriate answer (A, B, C or D).

Doctor Who

Doctor Who is **(1)**_____ regarded as one of the UK's most successful TV shows. It ran from 1963 until 1989, then returned to great **(2)**_____ in 2005.

The Doctor is an adventurer who **(3)**_____ from his home planet with a stolen time machine. One **(4)**_____ of the show is that the Doctor regenerates instead of dying, giving the BBC a chance to change actor every few years. There have now been thirteen Doctors.

One of the show's iconic **(5)**_____ is the TARDIS, the Doctor's time machine, which has two oddities. First, it is bigger on the inside than it is on the outside. Second, it resembles an early 1960s police telephone box. **(6)**_____, they had made a dull blue box a national treasure.

The Doctor's most famous foes are the Daleks, evil pepper-pot shaped robots whose battle-cry 'EX-TERMINATE!' is widely **(7)**_____ by school-children at playtime. The show's continuing high ratings means the BBC is **(8)**_____ to exterminate the Doctor any time soon.

1	**A**	broadly	**B**	strongly	**C**	widely	**D**	highly
2	**A**	acclaim	**B**	kudos	**C**	honour	**D**	commendation
3	**A**	deserted	**B**	absconded	**C**	hightailed	**D**	broke
4	**A**	strange	**B**	oddity	**C**	peculiarity	**D**	distinction
5	**A**	characteristics	**B**	features	**C**	aspects	**D**	attributes
6	**A**	Unwittingly	**B**	Erroneously	**C**	Meaninglessly	**D**	Thoughtlessly
7	**A**	mimicked	**B**	mimed	**C**	made	**D**	fabricated
8	**A**	improbable	**B**	unlikely	**C**	irresponsible	**D**	disliking

For questions 9–16, read the text below and decide which word best fits each gap. Use only one word for each gap. In the separate answer sheet, write your answers in capital letters, using one box per letter.

The ambush of Jess and Steven

"Hush," she whispered to Steven, her younger brother, as they scrambled (9)_____ the steep stairs. They suspected that they had heard someone upstairs but wouldn't be sure until they had investigated for (10)_____ and (11)_____ their own eyes upon him or her.

The creak of the bedroom door must have (12)_____ them away, because no (13)_____ had they crept into their parent's bedroom when Dad jumped out! Jess screamed at the (14)_____ of her voice, and then laughed uncontrollably, falling to the floor as Dad tickled her. Steven wasn't much help. By that point he was bouncing on the big bed, trying to do a somersault and (15)_____ on his feet again.

The bubble burst as Mum came in to the bedroom and gave everyone a good telling off. Dad, Jess and Steven fell quickly into line, standing to attention as Mum read them all the riot (16)_____ and told them all how silly they had been.

For questions 17–24, use the stem word on the right to form the correct word that fills each gap. In the separate answer sheet, write your answers in capital letters, using one box per letter.

Olive oil

Italy is **(17)**_____ an olive oil crisis as olive harvests are declining rapidly. In 2018 a **(18)**_____ mix of spring frosts, a very dry summer and a rainy autumn caused a record low crop. The cost to the Italian economy was, by some economist's **(19)**_____, one billion euros. The cost to national pride may be even worse – if the **(20)**_____ trend continues, Italy may need to turn to neighbouring countries to buy enough oil to meet its domestic demand. The history of olive oil in Italy goes back four thousand years, and the nation is proud of its characteristic **(21)**_____ (graced by more than 200 million trees).

GO

DISASTER

APPROXIMATE

DOWN

LAND

The freak weather conditions of 2018 were attributed to climate change, but nature also played a part. There was a plague of flies that laid their eggs inside olives, making them completely **(22)**_____ for oil production.

USE

Another invisible foe **(23)**_____ looms – the bacterium *Xylella fastidiosa* – which has killed hundreds of thousands of olive trees. The die-off began in the important olive-producing region of Puglia (which used to produce 50% of Italy's oil), but is spreading north quickly.

THREAT

(24)_____, the disaster is impacting consumers outside Italy, with a 30% price increase on bottled oil. Although other countries continue to enjoy good harvests, overall, olive oil is generally becoming more and more scarce.

DOUBT

For questions 25–30, complete the second sentence, using the word given, so that it has a similar meaning to the first sentence. Do not change the word provided and use between three and eight words in total. In the separate answer sheet, write your answers in capital letters, using one box per letter.

25 "Do not be deceived by the thieves' trickery," the master warned his students.

    TAKEN

    The master warned his students _____ trickery.

26 I do not intend to make the same mistake again.

    NO

    I _____ same mistake again.

27 I doubt that we will be able to persuade the bank to lend us the money.

    CHANCE

    I think _____ the bank to lend money to us.

28 My two brothers don't trust each other at all.

    COMPLETE

    There's _____ my two brothers.

29 Those people who waited outside for hours and who didn't get a ticket deserve some consideration.

    SPARE

    You should _____ waited for hours and didn't get a ticket.

30 His work didn't meet the standards that were considered acceptable.

    CONFORM

    His work _____ considered acceptable standards.

Answer sheet: Cambridge C2 Proficiency
Use of English

Test No. ☐

Mark out of 36 ☐

Name _____   **Date** _____

Part 1: Multiple choice

8 marks

Mark the appropriate answer (A, B, C or D).

0	A	B	C	D

1	A	B	C	D		5	A	B	C	D
2	A	B	C	D		6	A	B	C	D
3	A	B	C	D		7	A	B	C	D
4	A	B	C	D		8	A	B	C	D

Part 2: Open cloze

8 marks

Write your answers in capital letters, using one box per letter.

0	B	E	C	A	U	S	E				

9											
10											
11											
12											
13											
14											
15											
16											

Part 3: Word formation

8 marks

Write your answers in capital letters, using one box per letter.

17

18

19

20

21

22

23

24

Part 4: Key word transformation

12 marks

Write your answers in capital letters, using one box per letter.

25

26

27

28

29

30

Cambridge C2 Proficiency Use of English

Test 7

For questions 1–8, read the text below and decide which answer best fits each gap. In the separate answer sheet, mark the appropriate answer (A, B, C or D).

Clever Crows – the most intelligent birds?

Crows have yet again **(1)**_____ scientists with their remarkable problem-solving skills. A group of New Caledonian crows was presented with a problem in which food was placed in a passageway too narrow for their beaks to access. However, four out of eight birds **(2)**_____ put together two short sticks located nearby to make a longer fishing rod-type device to enable them to reach the food. In the wild, crows have been known to also use leaves, rocks and even their own feathers to **(3)**_____ otherwise impossible tasks. They even craft and use hooks to **(4)**_____ insects.

How intelligence evolves was studied in one cleverly-designed experiment when birds were **(5)**_____ to use a kind of vending machine to **(6)**_____ rewards. By studying the birds' cognitive abilities, the researchers hope that their **(7)**_____ will help the development of Artificial Intelligence (AI) technology. Presented with these tasks, **(8)**_____ anything crows would come upon in nature, scientists showed how the birds adapted their own instinctual behaviour to complete the fabricated tests.

1	**A** confounded	**B** fazed	**C** perturbed	**D** distracted
2	**A** freely	**B** unconsciously	**C** spontaneously	**D** willingly
3	**A** facilitate	**B** alleviate	**C** abridge	**D** promote
4	**A** arrest	**B** corral	**C** snare	**D** seduce
5	**A** propelled	**B** caused	**C** induced	**D** prompted
6	**A** accomplish	**B** gain	**C** reap	**D** glean
7	**A** findings	**B** acquisitions	**C** attainments	**D** fallout
8	**A** different	**B** contrary	**C** unlike	**D** distinct

For questions 9–16, read the text below and decide which word best fits each gap. Use only one word for each gap. In the separate answer sheet, write your answers in capital letters, using one box per letter.

The lightbulb

In 1879 the first commercially practical incandescent light was introduced to the market by Thomas Alva Edison. However, he was neither the first **(9)**_____ the only person trying to invent an incandescent light bulb. In fact, it is claimed by some historians that there were over 20 inventors of incandescent lamps prior to Edison's version, yet Edison is often credited **(10)**_____ the invention because his invention outdid the earlier versions due to an effective, high-resistance material, which made power distribution from a centralised source more economically viable, achieving a better vacuum within the bulb. This combination of features set Edison's bulb apart **(11)**_____ the competitors who had come before.

Humphry Davy invented the first electric light in 1802. Connected to a battery and using a piece of carbon as a filament, the device glowed, but not for long, and was much **(12)**_____ bright for practical use. In 1840 Warren de la Rue introduced a vacuum tube and passed an electric current **(13)**_____ it.

In 1850 Joseph Wilson Swan came up **(14)**_____ the name and idea of a 'light bulb', enclosing carbonised paper filaments in an evacuated glass bulb, and by 1860 had a working prototype. However, in the 1870s, better vacuum pumps became available and Swan continued with his experiments until, in 1878, he developed a **(15)**_____ lasting light bulb using a treated cotton thread. In 1874 a patent was filed by other inventors – Henry Woodward and Mathew Evans. They eventually sold their patent to Edison in 1879, who went **(16)**_____ to develop, perfect and mass-produce light bulbs.

For questions 17–24, use the stem word on the right to form the correct word that fills each gap. In the separate answer sheet, write your answers in capital letters, using one box per letter.

The Employment Acts of 1980 and 1982

With inflation in the United Kingdom peaking at 22% in 1980, and **(17)**_____ reaching an **EMPLOY**
(18)_____ three million by January 1982 **PRECEDENT**
(12.1% of the working population), a period of dramatic technological change saw the entire British manufacturing industry slowing down and
(19)_____ disintegrate: economic recession **EFFECT**
on a global scale, cuts in educational funding, restrictions in library budgets, and **(20)**_____ in the **CAPACITY**
manufacturing industry saw the demise of many long-standing British firms.

The introduction by the Conservative Party of the Employment Acts of 1980 and 1982, which narrowed the definition of a lawful trade dispute between workers and employers to matters mainly employment-related (for example, pay and work **(21)**_____) gave rise **ALLOCATE**
to vigilant yet ultimately futile union efforts to
(22)_____ the industry's domestic **FORTIFICATION**
employment situation. The British newspaper industry provides a stark instance of how desperate a time this was when, in 1986, and despite fierce union
(23)_____, the transition of production **RESIST**
methods literally occurred **(24)**_____. **NIGHT**

For questions 25–30, complete the second sentence, using the word given, so that it has a similar meaning to the first sentence. Do not change the word provided and use between three and eight words in total. In the separate answer sheet, write your answers in capital letters, using one box per letter.

25   Not until Wendy had arrived did Steven make his big announcement.

FOR

Steven _____ his big announcement.

26   The reason it has happened that way is a mystery to me.

LOSS

I am _____ it has happened like that.

27   I wasn't at all surprised when I heard that Sophie had been promoted.

HEAR

It came _____ Sophie's promotion.

28   The judge said that it was only because of the man's age that she had not sent him to prison.

HIS

The judge said that had it _____ sent the man to prison.

29   They didn't want to give up while some hope of success remained.

DEFEAT

They were loath _____ some hope of success.

30   The player described his childhood vividly in the interview.

ACCOUNT

When he was _____ his childhood.

Answer sheet: Cambridge C2 Proficiency Use of English

Test No. ☐

Mark out of 36 ☐

Name _____   **Date** _____

Part 1: Multiple choice

8 marks

Mark the appropriate answer (A, B, C or D).

0	A	**B**	C	D	

1	A	B	C	D		5	A	B	C	D	
2	A	B	C	D		6	A	B	C	D	
3	A	B	C	D		7	A	B	C	D	
4	A	B	C	D		8	A	B	C	D	

Part 2: Open cloze

8 marks

Write your answers in capital letters, using one box per letter.

0	B	E	C	A	U	S	E				

9											
10											
11											
12											
13											
14											
15											
16											

Part 3: Word formation

Write your answers in capital letters, using one box per letter.

17

18

19

20

21

22

23

24

Part 4: Key word transformation

Write your answers in capital letters, using one box per letter.

25

26

27

28

29

30

PROSPERITY EDUCATION
www.prosperityeducation.net

Cambridge C2 Proficiency Use of English

Test 8

For questions 1–8, read the text below and decide which answer best fits each gap. In the separate answer sheet, mark the appropriate answer (A, B, C or D).

Producing and printing books

Book production at Cambridge University Press, the world's oldest publisher and longest continual printer, has evolved with the industry, adapting at its **(1)**_____ to successive technological shifts throughout a four-hundred-year manufacturing **(2)**_____. Perhaps surprisingly, given such a **(3)**_____ period of time, there have been just two major changes to the process by which text is prepared **(4)**_____ to being mechanically printed to paper.

Johannes Gutenburg's publishing innovation of 1450, by which the setting of individual characters of metal type in devices called 'braces' or 'matrices' **(5)**_____ for the first time the **(6)**_____ of printed sheets of text, and remained until the second half of the nineteenth century the fundamental production standard.

The introduction of phototypesetting in the 1950s and the increasing popularity **(7)**_____ the publishing industry of printing by offset lithography saw an end to almost half a millennium of letterpress typesetting as the **(8)**_____ service offered by Cambridge University Press.

1	A	forethought	B	forerunner	C	forefront	D	foremost
2	A	legacy	B	estate	C	leftover	D	inheritance
3	A	profound	B	vast	C	far-reaching	D	gigantic
4	A	before	B	anterior	C	former	D	prior
5	A	enabled	B	empowered	C	permitted	D	ensured
6	A	discovery	B	introduction	C	evolution	D	proliferation
7	A	across	B	over	C	under	D	upon
8	A	fundamental	B	primary	C	underlying	D	elementary

For questions 9–16, read the text below and decide which word best fits each gap. Use only one word for each gap. In the separate answer sheet, write your answers in capital letters, using one box per letter.

The Portable Document Format

You have, without doubt, seen or used the document format about which you are going to read. **(9)**_____ it was released in 1994, Adobe's PDF, which was initially developed for the office environment, quickly became the tool of **(10)**_____ for designers and graphical artists everywhere. The world, and in particular, business (and therefore the office world) is jam-packed with names of organisations such as 'NASA' and 'UNICEF'. There are even expressions that we abbreviate to make them quicker to say ('ASAP' springs to **(11)**_____).

(12)_____ everyone knows that the acronym PDF means 'Portable Document Format', so it is quite okay to refer to the document as 'a PDF file'. A succinct definition is that 'PDF' is a file format for representing documents in a standardised way, **(13)**_____ of the application software, hardware, and operating system used to create them.

This means, essentially, that however the original material is presented, once that content has been converted to PDF, the original presentation will be retained. It's hard to appreciate quite **(14)**_____ revolutionary this invention was, but it's **(15)**_____ harder to imagine a world without it. It has become ubiquitous in the office and in all walks of **(16)**_____, even if the exact meaning of the acronym might sometimes be misunderstood.

For questions 17–24, use the stem word on the right to form the correct word that fills each gap. In the separate answer sheet, write your answers in capital letters, using one box per letter.

The Spanish Flu

The Spanish Flu (17)_____ of 1918 was one of the worst pandemics the modern world has ever known, and is said to have claimed more lives than the (18)_____ First World War, which ended the same year.   **BREAK**

CATASTROPHE

That particular virus was so called not because it started in Spain. Due to the fact that none of the (19)_____ in that most terrible of conflicts at the time wanted to admit they had such a problem ravaging the population, in case it was seen as a sign of weakness, the news went (20)_____. Spain was neutral in the War and had no reason to hide the news of the devastating illness. So, the virus was first reported there, and hence, Spain, rather (21)_____, gave this particular flu its name.   **PARTICIPATE**

REPORT

FAIR

The Spanish Flu spread to every corner of the world, with reports of the decimation of communities in places such as Western Samoa and Alaska. (22)_____ compiled estimations state that at least 50 million – perhaps as many as 100 million – people died as a result.   **SCIENCE**

To put that in context – in the four years of the First World War, an estimated 16 million military (23)_____ lost their lives, and it is estimated a (24)_____ total of 37 million people died as a result of the conflict. Still, the total deaths related to The Spanish Flu far exceeded that terrible number.   **PERSON**

STAGGER

For questions 25–30, complete the second sentence, using the word given, so that it has a similar meaning to the first sentence. Do not change the word provided and use between three and eight words in total. In the separate answer sheet, write your answers in capital letters, using one box per letter.

25   The company is rumoured to have lost a huge amount of money in the past year because of fierce competition.

   SUSTAINED

   Apparently the company has _____ to fierce competition.

26   Mr Smith asked if the client minded if he started things off.

   OBJECTION

   "Do you have _____ rolling?" asked Mr Smith

27   Mrs Smart was well known as a bad-tempered person.

   REPUTATION

   Mrs Smart's _____ well known.

28   So that he would be able to leave the room quickly, Mathew stood by the door.

   POSITIONED

   Mathew _____ to be able to leave the room quickly.

29   It had been a terrible day, but I cheered up when I saw my kids again.

   SIGHT

   After a terrible day my spirits _____ of my kids again.

30   Do you have any idea how Sarah managed to make the money she needed to buy that house?

   LIGHT

   Can _____ enough money to buy that house?

Answer sheet: Cambridge C2 Proficiency Use of English

Test No. ☐

Mark out of 36 ☐

Name _____ **Date** _____

Part 1: Multiple choice

8 marks

Mark the appropriate answer (A, B, C or D).

| 0 | A | **B** | C | D | |

1	A	B	C	D			5	A	B	C	D	
2	A	B	C	D			6	A	B	C	D	
3	A	B	C	D			7	A	B	C	D	
4	A	B	C	D			8	A	B	C	D	

Part 2: Open cloze

8 marks

Write your answers in capital letters, using one box per letter.

| 0 | B | E | C | A | U | S | E | | | | |

9										
10										
11										
12										
13										
14										
15										
16										

Part 3: Word formation

8 marks

Write your answers in capital letters, using one box per letter.

17 ☐☐☐☐☐☐☐☐☐☐☐

18 ☐☐☐☐☐☐☐☐☐☐☐

19 ☐☐☐☐☐☐☐☐☐☐☐

20 ☐☐☐☐☐☐☐☐☐☐☐

21 ☐☐☐☐☐☐☐☐☐☐☐

22 ☐☐☐☐☐☐☐☐☐☐☐

23 ☐☐☐☐☐☐☐☐☐☐☐

24 ☐☐☐☐☐☐☐☐☐☐☐

Part 4: Key word transformation

12 marks

Write your answers in capital letters, using one box per letter.

25 ☐☐☐☐☐☐☐☐☐☐☐☐☐☐☐☐☐

26 ☐☐☐☐☐☐☐☐☐☐☐☐☐☐☐☐☐

27 ☐☐☐☐☐☐☐☐☐☐☐☐☐☐☐☐☐

28 ☐☐☐☐☐☐☐☐☐☐☐☐☐☐☐☐☐

29 ☐☐☐☐☐☐☐☐☐☐☐☐☐☐☐☐☐

30 ☐☐☐☐☐☐☐☐☐☐☐☐☐☐☐☐☐

Cambridge C2 Proficiency Use of English

Test 9

For questions 1–8, read the text below and decide which answer best fits each gap. In the separate answer sheet, mark the appropriate answer (A, B, C or D).

The fourth industrial revolution

Many commentators now consider that we are on the **(1)**_____ of a fourth industrial revolution and that, by 2050, the world will be transformed in many fundamental ways.

AI (Artificial Intelligence) technology is creating machines that can not only process information much more quickly than the human brain, **(2)**_____ also learn from experience. Research in Robotics makes great **(3)**_____ forward every year. Increased functionality and miniaturisation means that robots are even being trialled in such 'human' areas as the service industry. Taking the healthcare **(4)**_____ as an example, it's now possible to predict a completely different experience for a patient ten years from now. Using machine learning and large data sets, AIs can already diagnose conditions from photographs or from the characteristic sound of a cough. Once diagnosed, patients might find they are treated by robots too. Robotic surgery is already **(5)**_____ in the United States, and robots that care for the needs of the elderly are already being used in Japan.

Of course, whether all this is positive or negative depends on your point of view. Some futurists predict that, rather than taking jobs, automation will simply remove the 'boring' parts – **(6)**_____ leaving humans free to **(7)**_____ more interesting work. Reduced working hours and commuting times could also be an outcome – leaving people more free to follow their own interests. And the **(8)**_____ increase in productivity will mean there is more wealth to support the young, the elderly and the unemployed.

1	**A**	edge	**B**	brink	**C**	fringe	**D**	frontier
2	**A**	though	**B**	so	**C**	and	**D**	but
3	**A**	strides	**B**	hops	**C**	lunges	**D**	marches
4	**A**	sector	**B**	area	**C**	division	**D**	field
5	**A**	customary	**B**	commonplace	**C**	obvious	**D**	humdrum
6	**A**	thus	**B**	furthermore	**C**	insofar	**D**	although
7	**A**	attend	**B**	chase	**C**	catch	**D**	pursue
8	**A**	total	**B**	overall	**C**	downright	**D**	complete

For questions 9–16, read the text below and decide which word best fits each gap. Use only one word for each gap. In the separate answer sheet, write your answers in capital letters, using one box per letter.

The richest person in history

Although Jeff Bezos and Bill Gates are super rich by modern standards **(9)**_____ is by any means the richest person of all time. In fact their huge fortunes are dwarfed by the wealth of Mansa Musa, the 14th-century West African ruler.

Born in Mali in 1280, Musa was born **(10)**_____ a dynasty of rulers. When his ruling brother abdicated in 1312, taking some 2,000 ships with him to find out what lay on the other side of the Atlantic Ocean, Mansa Musa ascended the throne.

Musa Keita I amassed a vast fortune from the plentiful resources found throughout his territory, such as gold and salt. His incredible wealth was, however, **(11)**_____ one part of his incredible legacy. He was a devote Muslim and **(12)**_____ such undertook his pilgrimage to Mecca in 1324. The sheer scale of the endeavour is breath-taking with reported figures of 60,000 soldiers, entertainers and other civilians, and as many as 12,000 slaves making up the enormous caravan. Musa lavished so much gold **(13)**_____ some places when he visited that he alledgedly de-stabilised their economies.

By the time he returned to Mali he had been elevated to near legendary status and his fame had **(14)**_____ to all corners of the world.

The Catalan map of 1375 depicted the ruler holding a sceptre and a gleaming gold nugget. **(15)**_____ today, mosques, mausoleums and libraries can be found as monuments that were built by the richest person who **(16)**_____ lived.

For questions 17–24, use the stem word on the right to form the correct word that fills each gap. In the separate answer sheet, write your answers in capital letters, using one box per letter.

Vlogging

If I'd told my parents that my career plan was to sit in my bedroom sharing **(17)**_____ videos on YouTube, they'd probably have had heart attacks!   **HOME**

(18)_____, there are thousands of   **SURPRISE**
YouTubers trying to **(19)**_____ build   **SUCCEED**
businesses. I get asked for advice every day. The problem with most YouTubers is that they treat vlogging like a hobby, not like a career **(20)**_____.   **OPPORTUNE**

So, here are the four pieces of advice I give to aspiring vloggers.

Collaborate, don't **(21)**_____. There's plenty   **COMPETITION**
of audience to go round, so why not work with other vloggers? **(22)**_____ brings benefits.   **OPERATE**

Get personal: Your audience likes you 'warts and all'.

Develop a work ethic: Vlogging is not your usual nine-to-five, but that doesn't mean it's not a job.

Get a manager: A lot of vloggers start young and find **(23)**_____ negotiating with big brands.   **SELF**

Follow these simple rules and you too could be an outstanding vlogger… maybe.

To be **(24)**_____, luck might be just as   **HONESTY**
important as working at it. So always have a Plan B.

For questions 25–30, complete the second sentence, using the word given, so that it has a similar meaning to the first sentence. Do not change the word provided and use between three and eight words in total. In the separate answer sheet, write your answers in capital letters, using one box per letter.

25   I should have had the car serviced last month.

    BETTER

    It _____ car serviced last month.

26   We must remember what age the woman is when we design her fitness routine.

    ACCOUNT

    A woman's _____ fitness routine is designed.

27   I thought Marina's original plan was to move to Spain.

    IMPRESSION

    I was _____ to move to Spain.

28   The officer thought it was an absolute miracle that no one was killed in the accident.

    SHORT

    The fact that they survived the accident was _____ officer's opinion.

29   The way you look at life would be greatly improved if you did some exercise.

    WONDERS

    A bit of exercise would _____ outlook on life.

30   There are often attacks by insects at this resort.

    PRONE

    This resort _____ by insects.

Answer sheet: Cambridge C2 Proficiency
Use of English

Test No. ☐

Mark out of 36 ☐

Name _____   **Date** _____

Part 1: Multiple choice

8 marks

Mark the appropriate answer (A, B, C or D).

| 0 | A | **B** | C | D | |

1	A	B	C	D		5	A	B	C	D
2	A	B	C	D		6	A	B	C	D
3	A	B	C	D		7	A	B	C	D
4	A	B	C	D		8	A	B	C	D

Part 2: Open cloze

8 marks

Write your answers in capital letters, using one box per letter.

| 0 | B | E | C | A | U | S | E | | | | |

9											
10											
11											
12											
13											
14											
15											
16											

Part 3: Word formation

Write your answers in capital letters, using one box per letter.

17

18

19

20

21

22

23

24

Part 4: Key word transformation

12 marks

Write your answers in capital letters, using one box per letter.

25

26

27

28

29

30

Cambridge C2 Proficiency Use of English

Test 10

For questions 1–8, read the text below and decide which answer best fits each gap. In the separate answer sheet, mark the appropriate answer (A, B, C or D).

Specs

Have you **(1)**_____ worn glasses? If you have, you'll **(2)**_____ appreciate how difficult life could be if you did not have the options to treat your sight problem.

The oldest image of glasses in existence is a 1351 painting of a Cardinal, though it is thought that, in around 1000 AD, we saw the **(3)**_____ of a contraption that took the form of a spherical glass and was used to magnify written words on a page. An Italian man was later **(4)**_____ with inventing wearable spectacles, in 1284. So, how did people with poor eyesight get by before then?

(5)_____ vision is an extremely common human problem, and it probably always has been. In fact, until relatively recently, glasses would have been beyond the financial capacity of most people. Surely the hunter or warrior would be **(6)**_____ affected by such an affliction. If the ability to read has not always been a priority, the ability to care for yourself has. It **(7)**_____ the question as to the extent of the problem in the developing world.

The next time we open our eyes, perhaps we shouldn't take how we see the world for **(8)**_____.

1	**A** never	**B** ever	**C** had	**D** been
2	**A** undoubtedly	**B** unexpectedly	**C** unsurely	**D** indescribably
3	**A** coming	**B** evolution	**C** advent	**D** discovery
4	**A** credited	**B** reimbursed	**C** blamed	**D** attributed
5	**A** Wasting	**B** Deteriorating	**C** Regressing	**D** Corroding
6	**A** drastically	**B** really	**C** completely	**D** remarkably
7	**A** supplicates	**B** begs	**C** asks	**D** makes
8	**A** granted	**B** given	**C** sure	**D** ride

For questions 9–16, read the text below and decide which word best fits each gap. Use only one word for each gap. In the separate answer sheet, write your answers in capital letters, using one box per letter.

Working from home

Whenever I tell someone that I work from home, nine times out of ten they will make a joke **(9)**_____ how much television I must watch, or how many naps I must **(10)**_____ instead of working. Usually, they will comment that they couldn't do it **(11)**_____ as they lack the self-discipline. In my experience, **(12)**_____ worked from home for several years now, discipline doesn't come **(13)**_____ the equation.

If you have to earn money, which I do, then you will work as hard as you possibly can to do so. I barely have time to **(14)**_____ a breath during my day, such is the amount of work I must do, and, at times, it does get lonely, but I wouldn't work in an office again, that's for sure. The freedom I'm afforded **(15)**_____ being my own boss far outweighs any benefits for which you might be eligible when working for a company.

But when I am asked how I ever manage to get any work done with all the distractions that **(16)**_____ with being at home, I just laugh and say 'It's okay, my boss is very understanding'.

For questions 17–24, use the stem word on the right to form the correct word that fills each gap. In the separate answer sheet, write your answers in capital letters, using one box per letter.

Banksy – street artist *extraordinaire*

Banksy's **(17)**_____ spontaneous creations began **(18)**_____ up in urban areas – namely Bristol and then London, England. The works by the anonymous street artist have turned him into the hippest and most highly **(19)**_____ after artist working today.

SEEM

POP

SEEK

He is a **(20)**_____ name all over the world. His works have transcended the art gallery, appealing to the common man, before making their way back into the auction rooms of the world and raising huge sums.

HOUSE

His **(21)**_____ street art is executed using a distinctive stenciling technique. The politically charged work is in fact a social **(22)**_____, and has often appeared on walls, bridges and self-built props throughout the world.

SATIRE

COMMENT

His **(23)**_____ are regularly resold, albeit sometimes by actually removing the whole section of wall on which they are painted. His work is at once extremely fashionable and **(24)**_____ acclaimed.

INSTALL

CRITIC

For questions 25–30, complete the second sentence, using the word given, so that it has a similar meaning to the first sentence. Do not change the word provided and use between three and eight words in total. In the separate answer sheet, write your answers in capital letters, using one box per letter.

25   "We'll leave first thing Tuesday unless Zara's plans change before Monday, I said.

      NO

      Provided _____ now and Monday we'll leave first thing Tuesday," I said.

26   George found it very easy to invent science-fiction stories.

      COMING

      George had no _____ science-fiction stories.

27   The detective reported that, as far as he knew, the suspect was not lying.

      SUPPOSE

      "I've got _____ the truth," said the detective.

28   She tried as hard as she could to make sure that this problem would not arise.

      POWER

      She _____ this problem from arising.

29   Marcus was offended when he was not included in the team.

      EXCEPTION

      Marcus _____ out of the team.

30   Tracey has finally accepted that their friendship is over.

      TERMS

      Tracey has finally _____ their friendship is over.

Answer sheet: Cambridge C2 Proficiency Use of English

Test No. ☐

Mark out of 36 ☐

Name _____ **Date** _____

Part 1: Multiple choice

8 marks

Mark the appropriate answer (A, B, C or D).

| 0 | A | B | C | D | |

1	A	B	C	D	
2	A	B	C	D	
3	A	B	C	D	
4	A	B	C	D	

5	A	B	C	D	
6	A	B	C	D	
7	A	B	C	D	
8	A	B	C	D	

Part 2: Open cloze

8 marks

Write your answers in capital letters, using one box per letter.

| 0 | B | E | C | A | U | S | E | | | | |

9
10
11
12
13
14
15
16

Part 3: Word formation

8 marks

Write your answers in capital letters, using one box per letter.

17
18
19
20
21
22
23
24

Part 4: Key word transformation

12 marks

Write your answers in capital letters, using one box per letter.

25

26

27

28

29

30

Answers

Part 1: Multiple choice

1	C	bears	5	B	Whereas
2	B	intents	6	A	stirred
3	B	perch	7	B	veritable
4	A	superseded	8	C	opening

Part 2: Open cloze

9	for	13	However
10	to	14	campaign
11	lay	15	time
12	without	16	rest

Part 3: Word formation

17	offspring	21	anatomical
18	strength	22	captivity
19	infertile	23	weighing
20	cross-breeding	24	Conservationists

Part 4: Key word transformation

25	there was a lack of	clarity when
26	it difficult / it more difficult	to reach
27	up hope of	winning the game despite
28	there is a strong	probability (that) it will / probability of / likelihood (that) it will / likelihood of / possibility (that) it will / possibility of / chance (that) it will / chance of
29	were justified in	making such
30	interference everything would	have gone smoothly

Part 1: Multiple choice

1	A	implausible	5	D	deep
2	A	pool	6	C	perks
3	D	imply	7	B	hearty
4	A	constitutes	8	B	winks

Part 2: Open cloze

9	say	13	means
10	norm	14	each
11	take	15	likes
12	such	16	taking

Part 3: Word formation

17	supposedly	21	mysteriously
18	relatively	22	existence
19	sightings	23	appearance
20	foremost	24	essentially

Part 4: Key word transformation

25	darkness fell did they	take the decision to / decide to
26	in the park is / here is / is restricted	unless
27	that the portrait bore	no resemblance to
28	had rained the concert	would have taken place
29	lot of problems	to contend with / with which to contend
30	himself to the possibility	of losing

Part 1: Multiple choice

1	B	pleading	5	C	conclusively
2	B	breadth	6	C	Decisive
3	A	combat	7	B	addressed
4	C	break down	8	A	Notwithstanding

Part 2: Open cloze

9	between	13	result
10	daily	14	fleets
11	instead	15	into
12	pick	16	idle

Part 3: Word formation

17	unkindly	21	countless
18	innovative	22	uncomfortable
19	insight	23	discoveries
20	born	24	obscurity

Part 4: Key word transformation

25	nothing I love doing more	than playing
26	the doctor's swift action	in calling the ambulance
27	is in danger	of becoming
28	made no reference / did not make reference	to the influence
29	of a sudden there was	a loud round / a round
30	taken note of my complaints	and would act / and would respond

Part 1: Multiple choice

1	A	stands for	5	B	embedding
2	A	credited	6	B	enabling
3	B	ultimately	7	B	generic
4	A	concerned	8	D	determined

Part 2: Open cloze

9	never	13	out
10	Take	14	After
11	about	15	both
12	step	16	on

Part 3: Word formation

17	soundtrack	21	versatility
18	outrageous	22	stylistically
19	recognition	23	innovative
20	breakthrough	24	philanthropic

Part 4: Key word transformation

25	shouted loudly the children	took no notice of
26	is every probability / is every chance / is every likelihood	it will rain / of rain
27	have a difference / share a difference	of opinion
28	us by surprise / us all by surprise	with her punctual arrival
29	instrumental in	the drafting
30	conducted herself	at the conference resulted in

Part 1: Multiple choice

1	D	subsequent	5	B	point-blank
2	A	cottage	6	A	advent
3	B	spare	7	A	budding
4	A	landed	8	C	Rather

Part 2: Open cloze

9	By	13	which
10	net	14	with
11	Due	15	without
12	subject	16	According

Part 3: Word formation

17	known	21	increasingly
18	Tragically	22	consequentially
19	misfortune	23	higher / high / heightened
20	prognosis	24	presently

Part 4: Key word transformation

25	had no choice	but to accept the decision
26	no account	are pupils to use the / can pupils use the / should pupils use the
27	not paying any / her not to pay any / not paying / her not to pay	attention to / any attention to
28	nothing I'd like / nothing I would like	more than to
29	you stuck to / you stuck by	what we originally / what we had
30	far as Susan is concerned	she has done

Part 1: Multiple choice

1	C	widely	5	B	features
2	A	acclaim	6	A	Unwittingly
3	B	absconded	7	A	mimicked
4	C	peculiarity	8	B	unlikely

Part 2: Open cloze

9	up	13	sooner
10	themselves	14	top
11	laid	15	land
12	given	16	act

Part 3: Word formation

17	undergoing	21	landscape
18	disastrous	22	useless
19	approximations	23	threateningly
20	downward	24	Undoubtedly

Part 4: Key word transformation

25	not to be / against being	taken in by the thieves'
26	have no intention of	making the
27	there is little chance	of persuading / of us persuading
28	a complete lack of	trust between
29	spare a thought for	those who
30	did not conform to	what were

Part 1: Multiple choice

1	A	confounded	5	D	prompted
2	C	spontaneously	6	B	gain
3	A	facilitate	7	A	findings
4	B	snare	8	C	unlike

Part 2: Open cloze

9	nor	13	through
10	with	14	with
11	from	15	longer
12	too	16	on

Part 3: Word formation

17	unemployment	21	allocation
18	unprecedented	22	fortify
19	effectively	23	resistance
20	overcapacity	24	overnight

Part 4: Key word transformation

25	waited for Wendy to arrive	before making
26	at a complete loss / at a loss	to understand why / to know why / as to why
27	as no surprise	to me to hear of / to hear about
28	not been for his age	she would have
29	to admit defeat	while there was still
30	interviewed the player gave	a vivid account of

Part 1: Multiple choice					
1	A	forefront	5	A	enabled
2	A	legacy	6	B	introduction
3	B	vast	7	A	across
4	D	prior	8	B	primary

Part 2: Open cloze			
9	When / After	13	regardless
10	choice	14	how
11	life	15	even
12	Not	16	life

Part 3: Word formation			
17	outbreak	21	unfairly
18	catastrophic	22	Scientifically
19	participants	23	personnel
20	unreported	24	staggering

Part 4: Key word transformation		
25	sustained huge losses	in the past year due
26	any objection to me / any objection to my	getting the ball
27	reputation for	being bad tempered was
28	positioned himself close to / positioned himself near to / positioned himself by	the door so as / in order
29	were lifted when / lifted when	I caught sight
30	you throw any light / you shed any light	on how Sarah made

Part 1: Multiple choice

1	B	brink	5	B	commonplace
2	D	but	6	A	hence
3	A	strides	7	D	pursue
4	A	sector	8	B	overall

Part 2: Open cloze

9	neither	13	on
10	into	14	spread
11	only / but /just	15	Still
12	as	16	ever

Part 3: Word formation

17	homemade	21	compete
18	Unsurprisingly	22	Cooperation
19	Successfully	23	themselves
20	opportunity	24	honest

Part 4: Key word transformation

25	would have been better to	have had the
26	age must be taken	into account when a
27	under the impression / under the impression that	Marina was originally planning
28	nothing short	of a miracle in the / of miraculous in the
29	do wonders	for your
30	is prone	to being attacked / to attacks

Part 1: Multiple choice						
1	B	ever	5	B	Deteriorating
2	A	undoubtedly	6	A	drastically
3	D	discovery	7	B	begs
4	A	credited	8	A	granted

Part 2: Open cloze			
9	about	13	into
10	take	14	catch
11	themselves	15	by
12	having	16	come

Part 3: Word formation			
17	seemingly	21	satirical
18	popping	22	commentary
19	sought	23	installations
20	household	24	critically

Part 4: Key word transformation		
25	there are no changes	to Sarah's plans between
26	problem / difficulty / problem in / difficulty in	coming up with
27	no reason to suppose	he is not telling
28	did everything in her power	to prevent / to stop
29	took exception	to being left
30	come to terms with	the fact that

Notes

Notes

Printed in Great Britain
by Amazon